WINDOWS 10

FOR SENIORS 2020/2021

The Complete Microsoft Windows 10 Guide for Senior
Technophobe with Latest Shortcuts, Tips & Tricks

James Jordan

LEGAL NOTICE

CONTENTS

CHAPTER THREE   55

THE WINDOWS 10 INTERNAL, EXTERNAL, AND CLOUD STORAGE   55

CHAPTER FOUR   76

MANAGING THE WINDOWS 10 APPLICATIONS
AND PROGRAMS   76

CHAPTER FIVE   83

MANAGING THE USERS ACCOUNTS   83

CHAPTER SIX   95

YOUR COMPUTER SECURITY IN WINDOWS 10

95

PREFACE

Windows 10 is the latest operating system invented by Microsoft Corporation. Getting yourself acquainted with this operating system can be a bit tasking. This user guide is prepared to aid your transition into this powerful operating system and to guide you step by step into maximizing the provision made available by this operating system. In case you are confused about how to get started on Windows 10, picking this book is the best decision you will be proud to make. I know Windows 8 has not been easy on you with the way it was configured. Don't worry; Windows 10 has come to lessen the burden.

With this book at your end, you will get to learn everything you need to know about Windows 10; what Windows 10 is all about, the new features added to it, and the requirement needed to get the Windows 10 installed on your computer.

You will learn how to use its features like the Start button, Cortana, the Taskbar, changing the background color and image, how to open multiple desktops on your window, etc.

In the course of reading this book, you will understand how the storage device on Windows 10 works and the tasks that can be carried out on it, and most importantly how to use the OneDrive.

The learning hasn't ended yet because you will learn how to manage your apps and program which involves launching, installing, and uninstalling them.

You are yet not left behind with the users' accounts. This is where you get to learn how to create a user account, how to change your password and interestingly you get to know how to open the Microsoft account.

Finally, you get to know some shortcuts, tips and tricks that will surely help you while getting busy with Windows 10.

With this in mind, what are you are still waiting for, c'mon let's take the ride together.

INTRODUCTION

Welcome to Windows 10. If you are familiar with Windows 8, I am sure you are already wondering what Microsoft Corporation is up to again. What surprises they have in stock for you with Windows 10. I know on the previous version which is Windows 8, there are some features that you were not expecting like the Start menu being taken away, thus, making it difficult for you to navigate through the Desktop environment. Don't worry; the start menu has been restored to Windows 10 thus making it convenient to navigate through the Desktop environment.

As at the time of this publication, Windows 10 is the current version of the windows available and it is used by billions of people at work, schools, home, and several other places that can't be mentioned. The truth is that Windows 10 is the best version of all other versions of Windows developed by Microsoft so far and the reason is that Windows 10 is the combination of Windows 7 and Windows 8 including additional features like the Cortana, Microsoft Edge browser, and other features alike. Can you now see why most people are getting their computers upgraded to Windows 10?

The windows 10 with the way it was configured can run almost any app or program on your computers and it has a catchy Graphics User Interface which makes it more enticing and interesting to use. You don't want to miss that right?

Hmmm, the truth is, if you are not used to the Windows from the scratch, you may have issues working with Windows 10 on

your device. To avoid this complexity, this user guide is made available for you; yes, I mean you! This user guide contains all the information that you need to know about the Windows 10 and how it can be used to get your desired result. Also, this user guide will save you the stress of calling IT personnel to help you get some things done using the Windows 10.

Therefore, join me, and let's explore this user guide together.

CHAPTER ONE

OVERVIEW OF WINDOWS 10

Generally, humans are ineffective without the brain and this is very much applicable to a computer; a computer is dead, or let's say dumb without Windows. I know you are wondering what a Windows is. Come on let's quickly talk about Windows generally.

What is Windows?

Windows is a collection of programs known as an *operating system* (OS) that controls and manages the activities that take place in a computer system. This operating system (OS) allows for the storing of files, running of software, playing games, watching videos, playing music, browsing the internet, etc. In a nutshell, Windows is what all other software or programs depend on the computer to function.

Windows was first developed by Microsoft Corporation on November 10, 1983, with version 1.0, and ever since then, other versions of Windows have been developed and with the current version to be Windows 10. Windows makes computer system user friendly by ensuring the provision for graphical display and organizing information in such a way that can be easily accessed by the users. The operating system makes use of icons and tools that help simplify the complex operations performed by the computers. According to researches made so far, 90% of computers use Windows *operating* system.

Importance of Installing Windows on your Computer

There are several benefits attached to the use of Windows and briefly, we are just going to highlight some of the benefits and they are as follows:

- Windows allows the users to interact with the computers with the use of hardware devices like keyboard, mouse, microphone, printer, etc.
- Windows helps to control the storage of data like images, music, and files on your computer.
- With windows on the computers, hardware devices like webcams, scanners, printers, etc. are attached to the computer.
- Windows allows programs installed on the computers to open and close and also create space out of the computer's memory that allows them to work effectively.
- Windows permit access by different users of a computer and at the same time ensure a maximum-security level of the computer.

- With Windows on the computers, a user can multitask by doing several things at once and such activities like watching of video and at the same time typing a document.
- Windows has an edge over the competition in the area of Plugs and Play support for computer hardware and also recognizing new hardware.

What's New About Windows 10?

Windows 10 is a series of operating systems developed by Microsoft and it is the successor to Windows 8.1. Windows 10 was first released on July 15, 2015, and to the general public on July 29.

Now let's talk about the new features added to Windows 10 that has made it different from every other version of Windows especially Windows 8.1.

- **Start Button and Menu**: The start button and menu which was removed from Windows 8 is replaced to Windows 10. The start button and menu has been expanded to locate important apps on the computer. Unlike using the Start screen to launch applications in Windows 8, you can now use the Start button and menu to launch applications in Windows 10

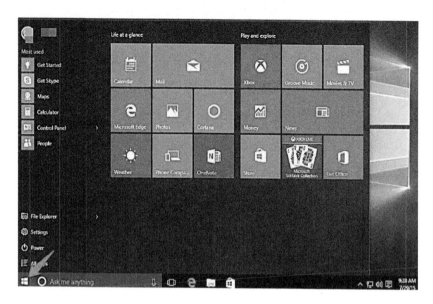

- **Apps on the Desktop**: Windows 10 lets you choose if you wish to run the apps on your computer on full screen or within your desktop windows.

- **Continuum:** This feature allows you to enlarge the Start menu and apps to fill the screen in such a way that is appropriate for finger touching on the screen especially on a tablet. When used on the desktop mode, the Start menu goes back to the normal size and the apps begin to run on desktop mode. The continuum feature gives your screen a smooth transition and a beautiful display. It is also developed to ensure that you get the best screen on your computer whenever it is on. Also, this feature allows you to switch from tablet mode to desktop mode and vice versa.

- **Cortana**: This is another feature of Windows which works exactly Start search just like in Window 7 or Window 8.1. This is a new digital assistant that can be controlled by voice. With Cortana, you can search for things on your computer, find files, checking for up-to-date traffic information about any location, get updated information from the internet, create and manage a list, set reminders and alarms, open apps your computer. The Cortana works from the Search box and it is located beside the Start button.

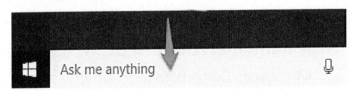

- **OneDrive**: This is another built-in feature of Windows 10, cloud storage created by Microsoft to allow you to save your important files remotely and secured in a place, and these files can be accessed anywhere. To use the OneDrive on Windows 10, you must be connected to your computer using your Microsoft account. With OneDrive, you can get your lost documents or files back using data recovery mechanisms that come with using OneDrive. This feature work like a traditional hard drive, but it's available through the internet with added features.

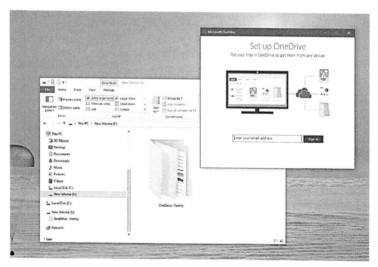

- **The Microsoft Edge Browser:** Another unique feature that came with Windows 10 is the Microsoft Edge browser which is a replacement of Internet Explorer which has been designed to give its users maximum satisfaction while surfing the internet. This app also comes with a new rendering engine called Edge HTML and it is also integrated with Cortana Digital Assistants which provides voice control, searches, and personal info to users. Microsoft Edge can compete with browsers like Chrome, Firefox, etc. with so many changes that have been made on it.

- **Multiple Desktops:** Another interesting feature about Windows 10 is that it allows you to create multiple or extra desktops instead of opening multiples windows on top of each other on the same desktop. You can set up a desktop to open your apps like video player and music and then switch to another desktop to open apps like Word, Excel, and Mozilla Firefox open. You can switch between them with a click or tab or you can hit the new Task View button on the taskbar.

To add a new desktop, all you need to do is click the Plus sign and this can be seen in the image below.

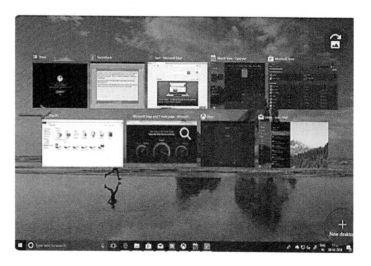

- **Unified Settings/ Control Panel**: Rather than of having two apps that control the device settings in the Control Panel and PC settings, Windows 10 has made it easier and less complicating y bringing them together in one piece.

Xbox App: Another added feature of Windows 10 is the Xbox used for game streaming with improved speed and graphics performances. Xbox app allows you to join your friends in games on Windows 10 or the Xbox Live.

Versions of Windows

Do you know that Microsoft has several versions of Windows 10? Guess you are surprised! Knowing and understanding what each version entail will help you know the version of Windows to get installed on your computer system.

Therefore, let's quickly discuss them.

- **Windows 10 Home**: This version of Windows 10 is aimed at the consumers' i.e. It is a consumer-focused edition that provides features like Cortana, the new Microsoft Edge web browser, continuum tablet, and desktop mode with other interesting application, etc.

- **Windows 10 Pro**: This version of Windows 10 is mainly developed for the small business market with features that help meet the needs of small businesses.

  It contains all the features of Home and it helps to manage devices and apps effectively and efficiently, protecting sensitive business information and also making use of cloud technologies for saving its data.

  Also, Windows 10 Pro helps to reduce management costs, provides a timely update for security, and also gives access to the current updates and innovations from Microsoft itself from time to time

- **Windows 10 Mobile**: This Window is designed for mobile touch screen devices like smartphones and tablets. This version enables its users to the Continuum feature, which allows them to use their mobile devices like a desktop when connected to a large screen.

  It has the same features as Windows 10 Home. Windows 10 mobile gives people who use their smartphones and smart tablets at work maximum productivity, security, and management capabilities.

- **Windows 10 Enterprises**: This is a version of Windows that is designed for large scale businesses and operation and provides tight security against threats aimed at devices, identities, applications, and highly classified and sensitive companies' information.

- **Windows 10 Mobile Enterprise:** Just like Windows 10 enterprise, it is designed for small large-scale business and solely meant to be used on mobile devices as the name implies. It is no doubt that organizations now use tablets for their day to day business.

- **Windows 10 Education:** This is designed to meet the needs of schools, colleges, and universities and it is made available through an academic Volume Licensing. This version of Windows is not offered to individual students for purchase.

- **Windows 10 S**: This is focused on internet-based processing that is designed or security and better performance while exploring Windows. It is designed to give faster boot times and longer battery lifespan. For security purposes, this Windows only allows apps from Microsoft Store and uses only Microsoft Edge browser for safe browsing.

The Windows 10 Hardware Requirement

Are you considering upgrading your pc from Windows 7 or 8 to Windows 10? It is expedient to know the necessary details or information needed to get the Windows 10 successfully installed on your pc and here I will be giving you the necessary requirements you must watch out for before installing Windows 10 in your pc.

Processor	1 gigahertz (GHz)
RAM	1 gigabyte (GB) for 32bits and 2 gigabytes (GB) for 64-bits
Hard Drive Space	16 GB for 32-bit OS 32GB for 64-bit OS
Graphics Card	DirectX 9 or later with WDDM 1.0 driver
Display	800x600

Internet Connection	Internet connection is needed to carry out update and downloads from time to time and to also get access to use some features that only available when the internet connection is on

CHAPTER TWO

GETTING STARTED WITH WINDOWS 10

Windows 10 Desktop

When you sign in to Windows, you are presented with the Windows 10 desktop. A desktop environment is an operation of the desktop allegory, made of a pack of programs running on top of a computer operating system which share a uniform graphical user interface. A desktop environment is sometimes described as a graphical shell. It is made up of windows, folders, icons, toolbars, wallpapers and desktop widgets.

Windows 10 Desktop Interface Explained

1. **Desktop Shortcuts**: this provides shortcuts to files, folders, and the Recycle Bin.
2. **The Taskbar**: Just like in earlier versions of Windows, the taskbar provides access to the Start Menu, shortcuts to programs, volume and date/time control, etc.
3. **The Start Button**: This can be found on the bottom left of your screen, the Start button lets you access computer programs and configuration options such as Windows Settings.
4. **Windows Search**: The Window search pane lets you search for programs, folders, and files.
5. **Task View**: This is a newly introduced feature in Windows 10 that gives you access to a task switcher tool along with a Virtual Desktop.
6. **File Explorer**: The file explorer is formerly known as Windows Explorer. The File Explorer is a file manager application that permits you to access files and folders on the computer.
7. **Taskbar Programs**: This provides quick access to opened or pinned programs.

The Start Menu and the Start Screen

The Start menu in Windows 10 is the combination of the features in the Start menu in Windows 7 and the features of the Start menu in Windows 8. The Start menu in Windows 10 shows the predefined contents while the Start screen shows the tiles.

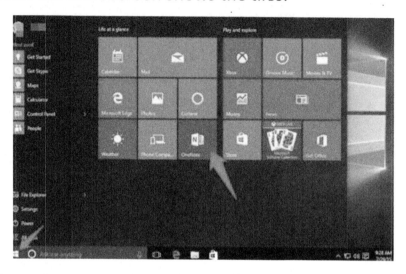

The Left Portion of the Start Screen

At the upper left-hand side of the Start Screen, the Start menu displays some items in which one of them gives you access to your account settings and with that, you can sign in, login in, or probably lock your account. Below this icon, is the quick access icon that enables you to access most-used apps and finally at the lower-left corner of the Start menu is additional items like File Explorer, Settings, and the Power button.

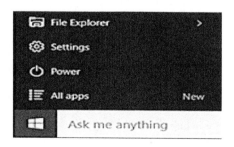

The Right Portion of the Start Screen

At the right-hand side of the Start screen, the Start menu displays the tiles attached to the Start screen and at the lower right-hand side of the screen are apps that are pinned to the taskbar.

Using the Start Menu to Launch the Start Screen

Do you know that there are two ways to display our Start screen using your Start Menu? In case you don't know, I will be listing them below:

- Press the Windows key on the keyboard

- With your mouse, move the cursor to the bottom left corner of the screen and click on the Start menu icon

Managing the Start Screen and Start Menu on your Windows 10

It is not enough that you know what the Start screen and Start menu are at the face level rather you must know how to manipulate these items to suit your taste. And for this reason, let's talk about how to find our way around the Start screen and Start Menu.

Working with the Start Menu

Resizing the Start Menu

You can adjust the size of your Start menu depending on your screen resolution and to get this done;

- Hover your mouse to the Start Menu and click on it for the menu to come up

- Move the mouse to the edge of the mouse, click and drag the mouse either up and down or left and right to make it bigger or smaller

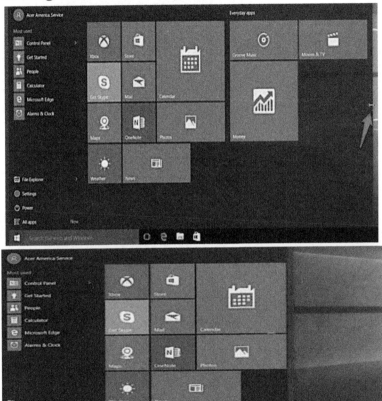

Launching Apps with the Start Menu

With Windows 10, you can easily access any app using the Start Menu and to locate them easily, all you need to do is;

- Click on the Start button and select All apps

- Scroll down the list to select any app you wish to launch

Note: You can also launch any apps by typing the name of the app in the search button beside the Start button

Pinning up your Favourite Apps to the Start Menu

You can pin your favorite to the Start Menu or for easy accessibility by doing the following

- Click on the Start button and select All Apps on the left side of the start screen

- Right-click on the app you wish to pin

- Select Pin to Start or Pin to Taskbar

- And the app will be pinned to the start menu

Unpinning apps from the Start Menu

In case there are apps you don't often use and you want to remove them from the Start, right-click on the app and select Unpin from the Start.

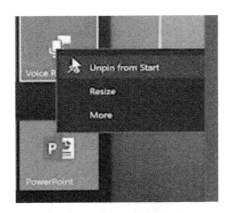

How to Display or Hide Apps List on the Start Menu

You can choose to hide or display your apps lists on the Start menu of your Windows 10. To do this;

- Go to Start Menu, type Start, and then click on the Start settings

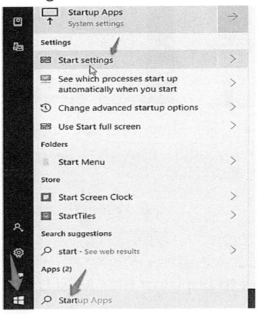

- Click Show app lists in the Start menu to turn off or on the app lists

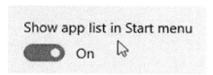

How to Display or Hide Recently Added Apps

- Go to Start Menu, type Start, and then click on the Start settings

- Click Show recently added app lists in the Start menu to turn off or on the recently added apps

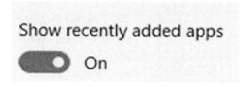

How to Display or Hide Most Used Apps

- Go to Start Menu, type Start, and then click on the Start settings

- Click Show recently added app lists in the Start menu to turn off or on the recently added apps

How to Remove or Add Folders on the Start Menu

You can add and remove whatever folder you wish on your start screen. To do this

- Go to Start Menu, type Start, and then click on the Start settings

- Select Choose which folder appear on the start screen

- Select the options that pop up and select the folders you wish to appear on the Start menu

Working with the Start Screen Tiles

One of the prominent features of the Start screen is the tiles and the tiles are square or rectangular and they take four different sizes which are small, medium, large, and wide.

Here we will be talking about how to use the tiles to give the Start screen the outlook or appearance we desire.

Resizing the Start Screen Tiles

You can adjust the size of the tiles to small, medium, large, and wide. To make this adjustment

- Go to the Start menu and right-click on any of the tiles you wish to adjust

- Click on Resize and choose any of the options you desire

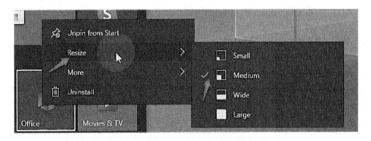

- The tile will be changed to the size selected

Removing the Tiles from the Start Screen

You can remove any tiles on the screen you don't often use or the ones you don't want to appear on the Start screen. To remove the tiles;

- Go to the Start menu and right-click on any of the tiles you wish to adjust

- Click on Unpin from Start

- And the tile is removed from the Start screen

Moving the Tiles within the Start Screen

You can also move the tiles within the Start screen and to get this done;

- Go to the Start menu, click and hold the tile and drag it to its new location

Creating a New Tile Group

You can create a group tile on your Start screen and by following the steps below:

- Go to the Start menu, select the area above a tile group

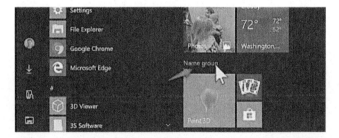

- Type in any group name and press enter

Renaming a Group Tile

If you want to rename a group tile;

- Simply select the group name

- Type in the new name and press enter

Note: *You can move group tiles by clicking and holding the new tiles and then dragging it to its new location*

The Desktop Environment

One of the essential parts of Windows 10 is the desktop environment. The desktop environment allows you to run several apps and programs together within the Windows. On the desktop, some icons give you quick access to frequently used programs, folders, and documents.

Right on the desktop environment is three major components and they are as follows:

- **The Start Button**: The Start button contains 80% of the desktop environment where almost all programs on the computer are located and launched

- **The Taskbar:** The Taskbar is located at the bottom edge of the desktop environment closely beside the Search box. The Taskbar contains apps that are currently opened and as well as containing icons to launch some applications that are frequently used.

- **The Recycle Bin**: The Recycle bin is a place where recently deleted apps are saved and they can be retrieved back to the computer system until they are permanently deleted. The Recycle bin is located in the upper part of the desktop environment.

Customizing the Desktop Background

You don't want to open your desktop environment and find the appearance appalling and uninterested. One of the interesting things about Windows 10 is that it contains some features that make the desktop environment enticing to use. However, you can manipulate the desktop environment by navigating to some places in your Windows settings. Therefore, let's take a tour to get your desktop customized.

Setting the Desktop Background Image

You can select just a background image or a series of background images.

To select one background image;

- Right-click on the Desktop screen and go to Personalize

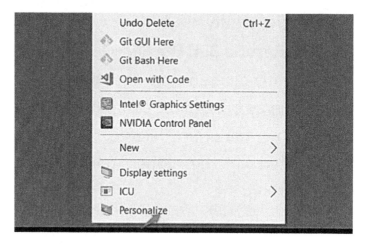

- Click on Background to select Picture

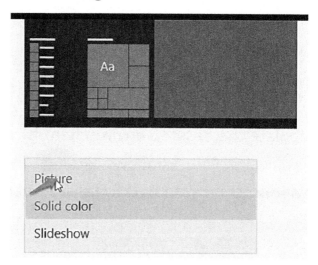

- A preview box will display, showing how the desktop background will look like

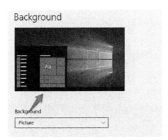

Note: *When choosing a background image, don't forget to always select Choose a fit list to be the Fill amidst every other option (Fill, Stretch, Tile, Center, or Span)*

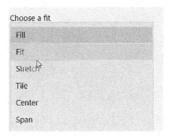

In case you want to upload a new image from your folder;

- Click on Browse and select the image you want from the folder. Then click on Choose this folder

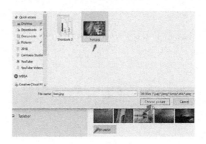

To select a series of background images;

- Right-click on the Desktop screen and go to Personalize
- Click on Background to select Slideshow

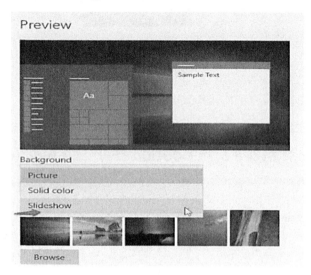

- Click on Browse and select the pictures you desire for the Slideshow. Then click on Choose this folder

- To change the duration of the picture, go to "Change picture every"
- To set the display of the folder content randomly, select the Shuffle toggle button to On
- You can select Fill, Fit, Stretch, Tile, Centre, or Span in the Choose a fit list to determine how the image will be displayed.

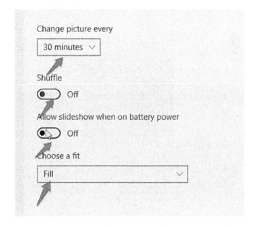

Setting a Desktop Background Colour

To set up the background color of the desktop;

- Right-click on the Desktop screen and go to Personalize

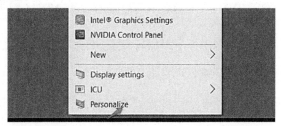

- Click on Background to select Solid Color

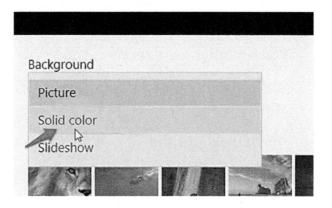

- Then choose any of the colors you like

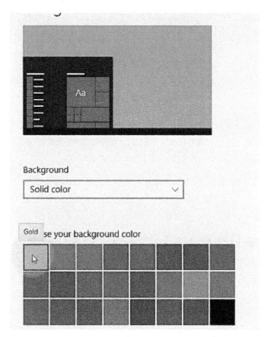

Creating a Custom Colour for your Desktop

Let's assume you don't find any color of your choice for your background; you can simply customize a color background all by yourself by doing the following:

- Click on the Plus sign beside the custom color

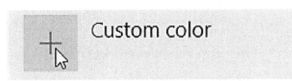
Custom color

- Choose any color by dragging the circle on the Pick a background color pop up screen

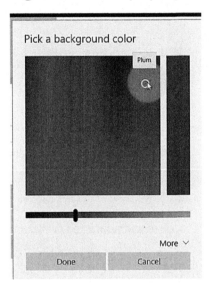

- Adjust the slide on the Pick a background color pop up screen to see the variation in the color

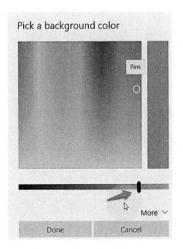

- To add additional colors, click on more, and select the necessary adjustment you wish to make. Then click on Done

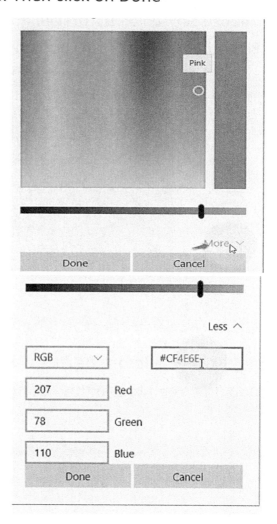

Toggling Between the Tablet Mode and Desktop

You can switch from your tablet mode to desktop mode depending on the mode you find suiting at any point in time. To achieve this;

- Click on the Action Center icon located on the Taskbar

- Then select the Tablet Mode button at the upper left-hand side of the Action Center pane

Note: You can switch from tablet mode to desktop mode by adding a mouse and a keyboard. The tablet mode works best with your fingertips while the desktop works best with a mouse and a keyboard.

Setting up Multiple Desktops on your Windows 10

In the previous Windows versions, you will have to get more than one monitor to have multiples desktops displayed. With Windows 10, you can open several desktops on a single monitor. These desktops are called virtual desktops and they allow you to switch from one desktop to the other.

To set up multiple desktops;

- Click on the Task View button on the Taskbar

- Then click on the plus above New desktop which is at the lower right-hand side of the screen

- In case you have some windows opened on the desktop screen and you wish to add them to a new desktop, right-click on them and select Move to New Desktop

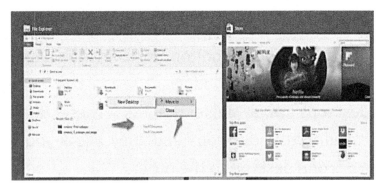

Working with the Taskbar

The taskbar is one of the most important features of the desktop screen and it is located at the lower edge on the desktop. The taskbar allows you to manage your apps and open your windows. The taskbar displays a button for apps that are pinned on it and it allows you to access them quickly.

How to Display the Taskbar Shortcut Menu

You can display the Taskbar shortcut menu by right-clicking on an empty area on the Taskbar

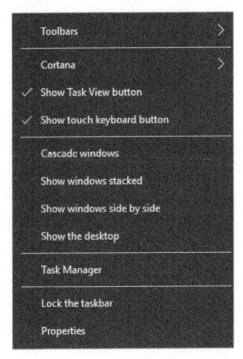

How to Pin the Taskbar to Any Position on the Desktop

The default location of the taskbar is at the bottom of the desktop. However, you can choose to change the location of your taskbar to left, right, or top and to do this;

- Right-click on an empty area of the taskbar and the taskbar shortcut menu will pop up. Then click on Taskbar settings

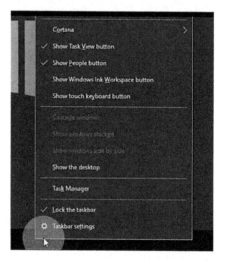

- Go to the Taskbar location on to choose you where you want the taskbar to be located

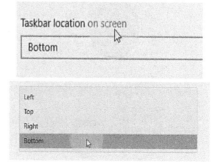

You can also move the taskbar to any location, by dragging the Taskbar to the desired location on the screen

How to Adjust the Taskbar Heights

To adjust the size of the taskbar, all you need to do is;

- Move the mouse cursor to the edge of the taskbar
- When it changes to a double-headed arrow, drag it to the desired height

How to Lock the Taskbar

Locking the taskbar helps to prevent changes to be made on the taskbar. To lock your taskbar;

- Go to the Taskbar menu shortcut and click on Lock the taskbar

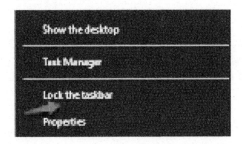

How to Hide the Taskbar

To hide your taskbar;

- Go to the Taskbar menu shortcut and click on Settings/Properties

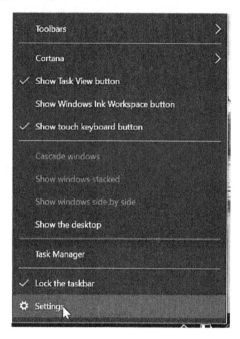

- Then click on Automatically hide the taskbar in desktop mode

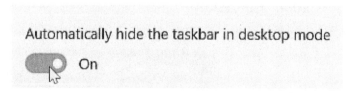

NOTE: *When you click at the edge where the taskbar is hidden, it will pop up and immediately you move your mouse cursor from it, it hides automatically*

How to Hide or Display the Task View Button

The task view button is an important feature needed to create multiple desktops on your Windows 10 and this icon can however be hidden or displayed from the desktop. To hide the task view button

- Go to the Taskbar shortcut menu and click on the Show Task View button

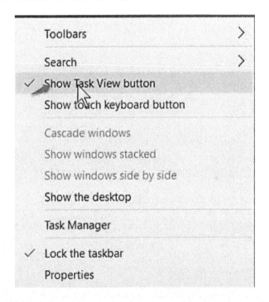

How to Display a Small Taskbar Button

Rather than using a big taskbar button, you can choose to display your taskbar button in a small form. To get this done

- Go to the Taskbar shortcut menu and click on Taskbar Settings

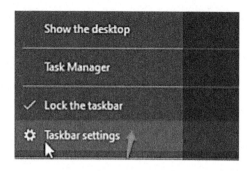

- Then select Use small taskbar buttons to turn on

Pinning up your Favourite Apps to the Start Menu

You can pin your favorite to the Start Menu or for easy accessibility by doing the following

- Click on the Start button and select All Apps on the left side of the start screen

- Right-click on the app you wish to pin

- Go to More and select Pin to Taskbar

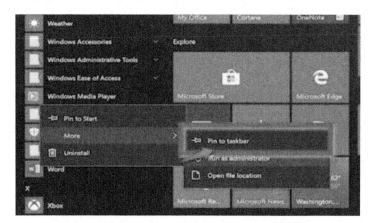

- And the app is pinned to the Taskbar

Closing Apps using the Taskbar

You can get your apps closed using the taskbar and to close any app running on the desktop screen

- Go to the apps opened on the taskbar and click on the X sign above it to get it closed

Working with the Cortana

Cortana is one of the features added to the Microsoft Windows 10. This is a new digital assistant that can be controlled by voice. The Cortana can search for files, apps, check for up-to-date information as well as getting information from the internet.

The Cortana is located on the Search box next to the Start button.

Here we will be talking about how to use the Cortana to get the desired result while working on Windows 10.

Setting up the Cortana

To set up the Cortana on your device

- Go to the Search box and type Cortana. Then click on the Cortana and Search settings

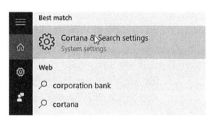

- Turn on the Cortana

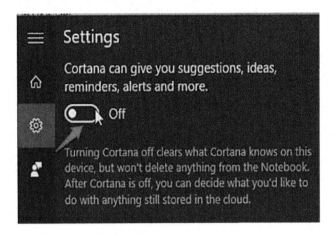

- Scroll down and click Use Cortana and then click on the Settings

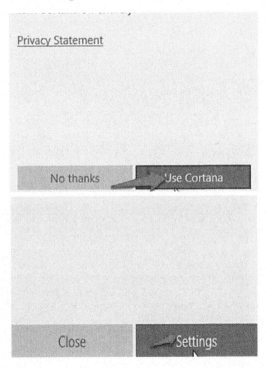

- Go to Region and language to add a language

- If any language is chosen is different from English, you will need to download the speech, and to do this, click on Options on the new language and go to download to get the speech it downloaded. When this is done, close the window and sign out.

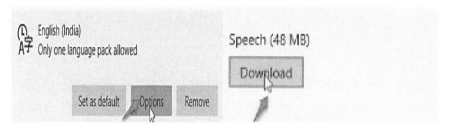

- Go back to the Start menu and click on the Settings

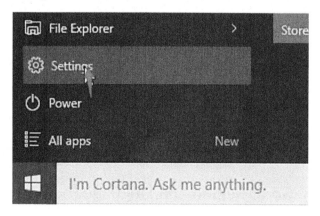

- Go to Time & language and select Region & language

 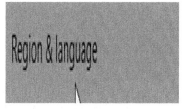

- Select the preferred language as the default language

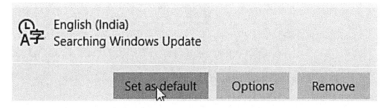

- Go to Speech and choose the language you speak to your device

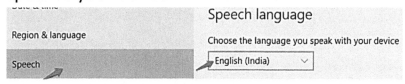

- Cancel the Window and then refresh to get started on the Cortana

How to Enable Hey Cortana!

Another interesting feature of Cortana is the ability to use the Hey Cortana. To enable this feature;

- Go to the Search box, click on Cortana and then go to Settings

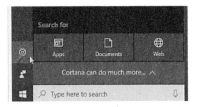

- Click on Check the microphone and a window will be displayed on the lower left-hand side of the screen and then click on Sure. The purpose of this is to ensure that Cortana can hear you

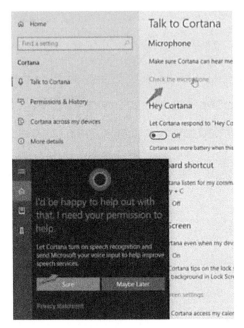

- Then turn on Let Cortana respond to Hey Cortana

Using the Cortana Notebook

The Cortana notebook is used to list things that catch your interest.

To use the Cortana notebook;

- Go to the Search box, click on Cortana and select the Notebook icon

- Then click on to do list to add anything on the Notebook

- You can also use the Manage skills icon to access other features on the Cortana Notebook

Cortana Learn my Voice

To enable the Cortana to recognize your voice

- Go to the Search box, click on Cortana, and select Settings
- Scroll down and click on Learn my voice

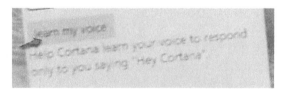

- Look for a quiet place and tap Begin

CHAPTER THREE

THE WINDOWS 10 INTERNAL, EXTERNAL, AND CLOUD STORAGE

Using the File Explorer

The File Explorer is an application that is used to manage and browse through files and folders on Windows. The File Explorer provides a graphical interface that allows users to have access to the drives, files, and folders stored on the computer.

There two major ways to access the File Explorer:

- Go to the Start menu and click on File Explorer

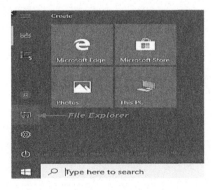

Or

- Go to the Taskbar click on the File Explorer

The File Explorer Window has some basic sections located on it and they are as follows:

- **The File Explorer Ribbon**: This is located at the upper edge of the File Explorer interface and the features on it look just like the features found in the Microsoft Office. This ribbon is used to perform common tasks on files and folders.

- **The Navigation Pane:** This is located at the left-hand side of the File Explorer interface that gives you access to your files and folders and the storage devices on your computer whether inbuilt storage device, any connected device or OneDrive through a list of shortcuts.

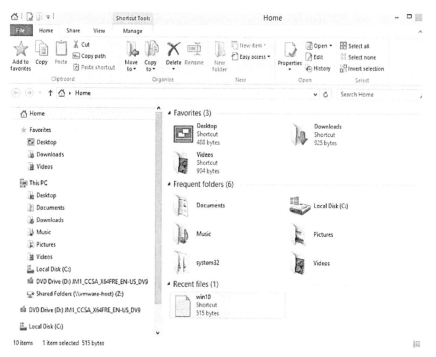

- **The Frequent Folder**: This is located at the right-hand side of the File Explorer interface that allows you access to files and folders that you have recently worked on
- **The Recent Files Section:** This allows you to access files and documents that you have recently opened. This is located at the lower part of the File Explorer interface

The File Explorer Ribbon

The File Explorer ribbons as earlier explained above is said to look like the features found in the Microsoft Office which is used for performing some common task on files and folders.

The File Explorer ribbon comes with four tabs with different commands. Now let's list some of the commands that can be performed by each tab.

- **The Home Tab**: This tab can perform the following task
  - Copying and pasting of files and folders

- o Moving of files and folders to another location
- o Deleting of files and folders
- o Renaming of files and folders
- o Creating of new folder and files
- o To check the Properties of a document or folder
- o Opening of files and folders
- **The Share Tab:** This allows you to share your files and folders using the options below
  - o Emailing or messaging a file
  - o Compressing a folder to occupy less space p
  - o Printing or faxing documents
  - o Sharing with other users or networks
- **The View Tab**: This tab allows you to make changes to the way Windows display your files and folders and the following changes can be made:
  - o Adding additional panes to view the details or preview of your files
  - o Changing of the files and folder from icon to lists as well as every other option available.
  - o Arranging and sorting the folders' contents

- o Hiding selected folders or files
- **The File tab:** This tab gives you access to a menu with different options listed below
  - o Opening extra File Explorer window
  - o Opening command windows for advanced users
  - o Configuring options on how File Explorer should work

Getting Accustomed to the Folders

One of the most important parts of the File Explorer is the Folder. A folder is a storage area where all your files and documents are stored and each folder carries a name for easy identification. There are six main folders found on your Windows (Desktops, Documents, Downloads, Music, Pictures, and Videos) and they are located in the Navigation Pane at the left-hand side of the File Explorer.

To locate any file or content in a folder, all you need to do is just double click on the folder.

Creating a New Folder

Imagine you save all your music, videos, and documents in a folder? No doubts, the folder will clumsy and tedious to locate any file in the folder. To avoid this stress, this is where creating new folders comes in handy. To create a new folder

- Right-click inside your folder and select New
- Select Folder and click on New folder that appears to type the name you wish to give to the new folder

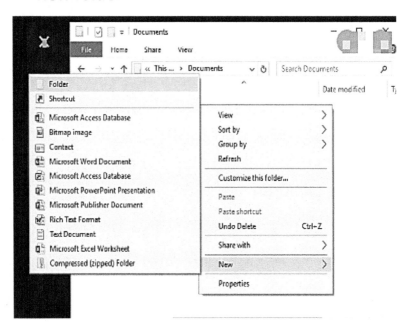

NOTE:

- *You can also create a new folder from the File Explorer ribbon. To do this, click on the Home tab and select New folder from the Ribbon. Here a folder will appear for you to type the name of the new folder*

- *You can also create a new folder from the Desktop, select New, and click on Folder. Then click on New folder that appears and type in the name of the new Folder.*

Renaming a File or Folder

Are you tired of a name given to your file or folder? It is very simple; all you need to is:

- Right-click on the folder or file
- Click on Rename and the old name will be highlighted in blue color. Then type the new name on it

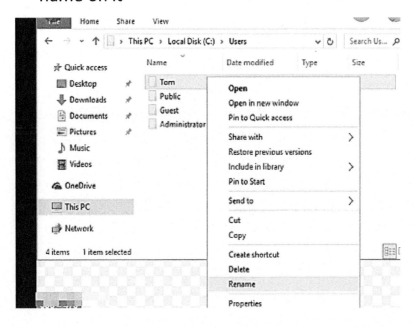

NOTE:

- *You can't rename a file or folder if the file or folder is currently in use. The only thing to do here is to close the program.*
- *When a file is renamed, the contents of the file do not change*
- *You can rename large numbers of files at the same time by right-clicking on the files, go to rename, press enter and all the files name will be changed.*

Deleting a Folder or File

There are times you will want to remove some files or folder from your Windows. All you just need to do is

- Right-click on the folder or file then select Delete

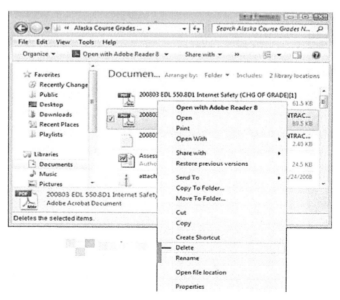

NOTE: *You can retrieve any file deleted from the Recycle bin but if you have deleted them from the Recycle bin, they cannot be retrieved again*

Copying or Moving Files and Folders

In case you want to change or move the location of your files and folders, you can choose to copy or move the files and folders

To copy files;

- Right-click on the folder or file to and copy
- Then move to the location you want to copy the files, then right-click and select Paste

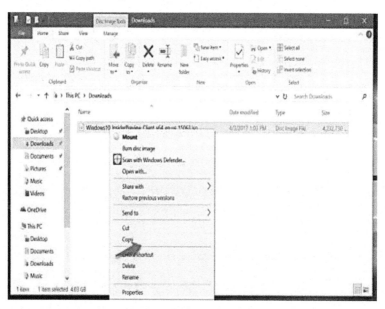

To move files or folders

- Place two windows beside each other

- Place the mouse pointer on the file or folder you want to move
- Hold down the file or folder and drag to the designated location
- Then release the mouse and the files will be pasted

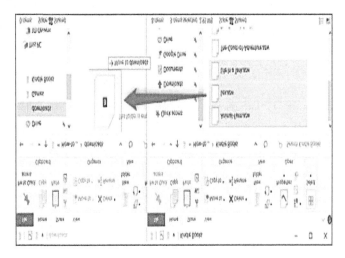

NOTE: *You can also use the Ribbon commands at the top of the File Explorer to copy or move files. Click on the Ribbon's Home tab and then select Copy To (Move to). Then select the location and then paste the files or folders there.*

Viewing More Information About your Files and Folder

When you create a file or folder, it contains some pieces of information that your Windows intentionally hides from you and they include information such as the size, location of the file, type of file, etc.

To view the more information about a file or folder

- Right-click on the file or folder
- Select properties from the popup menu and the information about the file or folder will be displayed

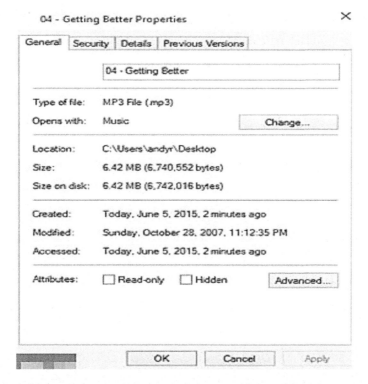

From the picture above, there are some pieces of information displayed in form of tabs and to have a clue of what they contain, let's quickly talk about them.

- **General:** This is the first tab that is displayed while checking your file properties and it shows information such as the size of the file, the programs that open it, and where it is located on the window.

- **Security:** With this tap, you can control the Permissions i.e. those who can access the files and what can be done with the files.
- **Details**: This tab gives explicit information about the files. For example, when showing details on songs, this tab displays the song's ID3 tag (MP3 or MP4), the name of the artist, the title of the album, the tracking number, the genre of the song, the length of the song, and other related information.
- **Previous Versions**: This tab shows the versions of this file that has been previously used and how they can be retrieved with just a click.

NOTE: You can as well view more information about your files and folders by using the View tab on the File Explorer ribbon. In the Layout group, click on details, and the details are shown in the picture above will be displayed for viewing

The CD and DVD Drives

The Disc drives are another part of the File Explorer that allows you to copy files and folders into a CD or DVD by using a method called burning. To locate the disks drive, open the File Explorer and at the right-hand side, you will see the disk drive. In case you are wondering what each disk drive mean, let's briefly talk about them to know how they operate

- **DVD –RW**: These can only read and write to CDs and DVDs
- **BD-ROM**: These can read and write to CDs and DVDs but can only read and not write Blu-ray discs
- **BD-RE**: These carry the same icon as the BD-ROM and they can read and write to CDs, DVDs, and Blu-rays' discs.

Copying of Files and Folders to a CD or DVD

You can copy your files and folders to your CD or DVD right from your computers. To do this;

- Put in the empty disk into the disc burner and then push in the tray.
- At the screen's upper, click on the Notification box that pops up
- Click on Burn file to a Disc option
- Type in the name of the disc and select Like a USB flash drive or with a CD/DVD player. Then click on Next

- Right-click on the items you want to copy and click on Send to. Then click on the disc burner from the menu.
- Here, a progress window pops up displaying the progress of the disc burner.
- When this is done, close the disc burning section by ejecting the disc.

Using Flash Drives and Memory Cards.

The flash drives and memory cards are the most commonly used external device storage on the computer. With the external storage devices, you can copy files from your computer or from your computers to the external drives.

The Memory Card: For the memory card to work, you will have to insert it in the memory card reader which will be plugged into the memory card slot on the computer. If the memory card reader is not used, the computer will not be able to access the file on the memory card. when the memory card reader is inserted into the computer, it appears like a folder on the File Explorer window. To open the memory card reader on your computer, double click on the folder

The Flash Drives: The flash drives work just like the memory card reader but the difference is just that it is inserted into the USB ports on the computer. To open your flash drive, double click on it

NOTE: *You can format your memory cards and flash drives with your computer and do this, right-click on the drives and select Format. Keep this in mind, once the memory cards and flash drives are formatted, the information on them cannot be retrieved again unless you have a backup for them.*

Using the OneDrive

Just imagine that your computer storage is filled and you have to store your files into your external storage devices like flash drives, memory cards, CDs, and DVDs. Of the truth, it will be so annoying especially when the storage devices got lost or damaged.

For this reason, Microsoft was able to proffer a solution to this by developing the OneDrive. OneDrive is an inbuilt feature of Windows 10 that allows you to save your files on the internet. This is your private file storage and it can be accessed anywhere even on other computers provided you have an internet connection.

When a file is changed on the OneDrive, the files automatically change on your computer and all other devices. You can as well access OneDrive from your phones or tablets.

To use the OneDrive on your computer, you need to have a Microsoft account and a strong internet connection. The OneDrive is located at the left-hand side of the File Explorer window.

Syncing the OneDrive Folders with your Computer

Syncing your OneDrive folder with your computer helps to automatically update any changes made on your files on the OneDrive to your computer. This helps to back up your files to the cloud and access them on your phones, tablets, and computers. When you don't sync a file on your OneDrive with a computer, any change made on that file will only reflect on your OneDrive and not on your computer.

To sync your OneDrive folder with your computer

- Open your File Explorer and select the OneDrive icon at the left-hand side of the folder
- Click on the Get Started button and sign in with your Microsoft account and password
- Click on Change location if you wish to change the location of your folders and if not, click on Next
- Select the files you wish to sync with your computer and click on Next

Adding Files to OneDrive

You can add your files from your computer to your OneDrive and to get this done, follow the steps below

- From the File Explorer, right-click on the files you wish to add then select Copy
- Go to the OneDrive folder at the left-hand side of the folder and open it
- Right-click inside the folder and select Paste for the files to be pasted into the One Drive Folder. (you can also drag the files to the OneDrive folder to avoid multiples copying)

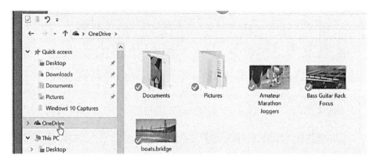

NOTE: Once your files are added to the OneDrive folder, the OneDrive automatically uploads your files to the OneDrive account online and you can now access them from the Internet.

Sharing of Files using OneDrive

One of the most interesting parts about the OneDrive is that you can share your files with other users using the OneDrive accounts. Not only that, you can as well share the files on your OneDrive with those who do not have a OneDrive account

- From the File Explorer, open the OneDrive to locate the files or folder you wish to share
- Right-click on the Files and select Share a OneDrive link

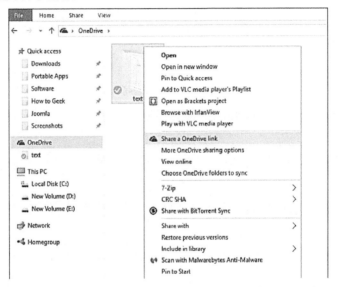

- A notification will pop up letting you know that a link has been created

- Open your email application and enter the email address of the person you wish to send the file to

- Go to the body of the email, right-click and paste the link
- Then select the Send button

Shared OneDrive File

B *I* U Aa A² A ∠ ≣ ≣ ⋧ ⋦ ≡ ≡ ≡ ∞ ☺

https://onedrive.live.com/redir?resid=FB7D92EA016572C8!81119&authkey=!AAkqbf930Ct ItA&v=3&ithint=photo%2cjpg

Configuring your OneDrive Settings

As you begin to get familiar with your OneDrive, there may be a need to make some changes on the OneDrive and you are perplexed about going about it. All you need to do is follow the steps below:

- Right-click on the OneDrive icon on the taskbar's notification area.
- Click on Settings and choose whatever changes you want to make on the OneDrive and then click on Ok

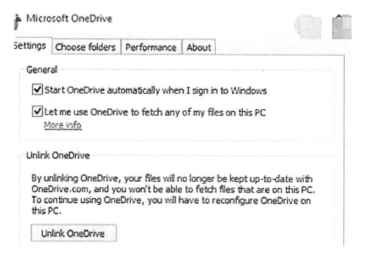

Accessing the OneDrive using the Internet

At times you may not be with your computer and you need to access some files on them and if you back them in your OneDrive, you can access them through any internet browser on another computer. All you need to do is

- Open your internet browser and type http://OneDrive.live.com
- When it opens, sign in with your Microsoft account name and password

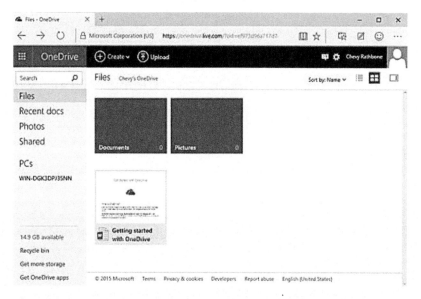

After signing in to your OneDrive on the internet, you can perform any operations like adding, deleting, moving, renaming of files, etc.

CHAPTER FOUR

MANAGING THE WINDOWS 10 APPLICATIONS AND PROGRAMS

Have you ever seen a house beautiful from the outside and only to get inside to realize that the house is not even close to being beautiful as the outside appears to be? I am sure you will be disappointed. That is exactly how your computer looks like without the apps and programs. It will be a boring device to work with.

The apps and programs are software that can either come with Windows or can be installed by the user himself. For the day to day running of your computer, it is the apps and programs that give it an adventurous appearance and here in this chapter, we will be discussing some basics of using these apps and programs.

Starting an App or Program with the Start Menu

To launch or start your apps and programs, the Start menu comes in handy. All you just need to do is

- Click on the Start button and go to All apps
- Scroll down the list to select any app you wish to launch

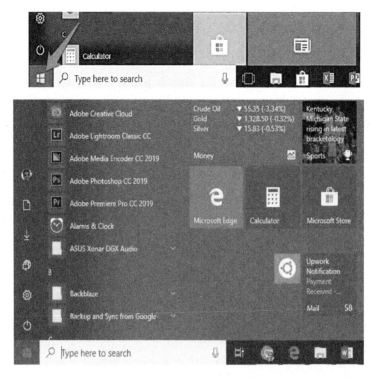

NOTE: *In case you can't locate an app or program in the All Apps, you can look for the app or program by typing the name on the Search box beside the Start menu.*

Choosing Default Program that will Open your Files

By default settings, Windows automatically select the program best suiting to open a file. All you need to do is double click on the file and windows will show you the right program to open the file. However, there are times the windows may not give you the desired program to open a file. Don't get yourself worked up, you can change the program to the one you desire, all you need to do is follow the steps below:

- Right-click on the file and select Open With from the menu that pops up
- Then click on Choose another app option.

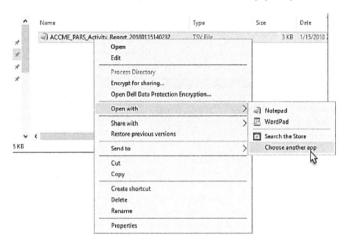

- Select the app you from Other options and then click on Ok

How do you want to open this file?

Keep using this app

Adobe Acrobat DC

Featured in Windows 10

Microsoft Edge
Open PDFs right in your web browser.

Other options

Google Chrome

Internet Explorer

Look for an app in the Store

☐ Always use this app to open .pdf files

OK   Windows

Familiarizing Yourself with the Windows Store

Just like Google Play Store is meant for Androids devices and Apple Play Store for iPhone devices. The Windows Store is also meant for Windows devices.

The Windows Store is an added feature of Windows 8 and 10. This is an online store to get Windows 10 apps for your computers. The windows Store helps to categories the apps on it for easy accessibility e.g. Business, Entertainment, Developer tools, Government and Policies, Health and fitness, Kids and Family, etc. For the Windows Store to work with your computer, it must meet the following requirements.

- A strong internet connection
- Screen resolution of 1024 x 768 and for Snap features the screen resolution must be at least 1280 x 800

To access the Windows Store, click on the Start menu and Select the Store app

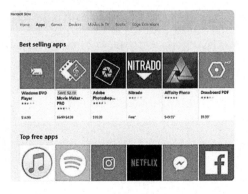

The cost of Apps on Windows Store

There are different costs attached to the apps on the Windows Store. However, they are categorized into three

- **Free:** These are apps you can get without paying a dime but they have limitations in their features. To enjoy additional features on these apps, you will have to upgrade to a paid version.
- **Trial:** These are apps with many features of a full paid version but can only be used for a short period.
- **Paid:** These are apps you get their full version and their costs start from 99 cents and several hundred dollars above. The more the cost of these apps, the more the features you enjoy.

Searching for Apps on the Windows Store

There are over a hundred apps on the Windows Store and going through these apps just to find a single app can be so stressful. That is why in the Windows Store interface, there is a search box at the upper right-hand side of the screen, where you type the name of apps for easy accessibility and installation.

Adding Apps from the Windows Store

Like we have rightly said at the beginning of this chapter that the Windows Store is where apps for windows are downloaded. Now let's quickly talk about how to get an app on the Windows Store

- Go to the Start menu and click on the Store app to launch it
- Go to the Search box to and type the name of the app

- The app will pop up with other related apps, then click on the apps
- Click on the Get button and the app automatically downloads and installs by itself

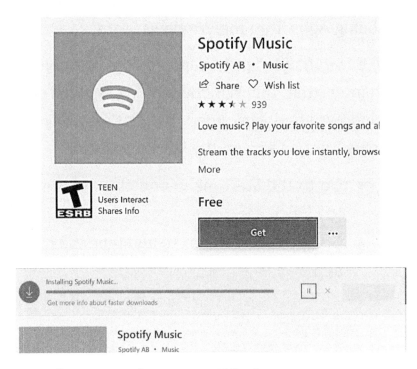

Uninstalling Apps from your Windows

You want to delete some old apps or there are some apps on your computer you need to do away with? All you need to do is right-click on the app from the Start menu and the Uninstall the app. The apps will be removed from your Windows. When you uninstall an app, the files and data associated with that app will also be deleted.

CHAPTER FIVE

MANAGING THE USERS ACCOUNTS

Everyone wants their space no matter how small it may be and no one loves their privacy to be intruded on. That is why in this chapter, we will be talking about user accounts.

The user account allows many users to use the computer without clashing each other. Each user can customize their desktop environments as well as other settings. Users can also create files and folders on their account right on a computer.

For Windows 10 to work after installation, it requires at least an account, and the first account is assigned to be the administrative account to manage the computer.

By default, in Windows 10, when the computer is turned on, login is required for the user to access the computer. You can log in by using a password, pin, or picture password.

How to Create a User Account

You can create more than one user account on your Windows 10 by simply follow the instructions below

- Go to the Start button and click on Settings
- Click on Accounts and go to Family & other users

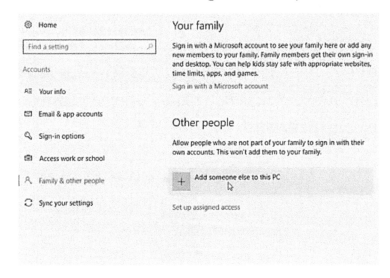

- Click on Add someone else to this PC
- In the pop-up screen, click on I don't have this person's sign-in information
- Here again, click on Add a user without a Microsoft account

- Here in the account registration pop up window, type the person's user name and password and reconfirm. Then click on Next to complete the account registration

Switching Accounts

Let's say you have several accounts on your computer and you wish to switch to another, all you need to do is

- Go to the Start button and click on the current user and select another account

Adding a Picture to your Users' Accounts

In case you feel the need to add a picture or change the existing picture from your user account to make it look attractive. It's simple, just follow the steps below

- From the Start menu, go to Settings

- Click on Account and move to the picture and select Browse

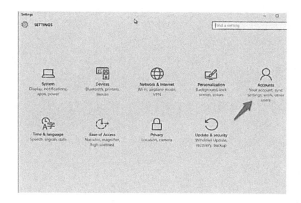

- By default, the picture folder is open and then selects any picture and click on Choose picture

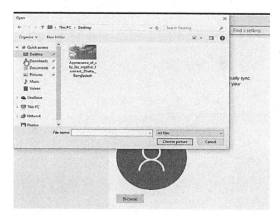

Creating a Strong Password

Creating a strong password is very important and this helps to prevent an intruder from opening your account to get some confidential information. To create a strong password, it must meet the following requirements

- It must be at least 8 characters
- It must not contain a real name, user account name, or any other name that can be easily guessed
- It must be a combination of uppercase letters, lower case letters, numbers, and symbols

Having this in mind, then let's proceed to how to create a password

- From the start button, go to Settings
- Select Account and go to the Sign in options
- Go to password and click on Add

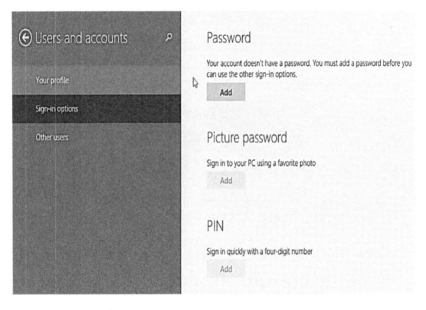

- Right on the Password page, enter and re-enter the password you will like to use and then enter your password hints (this is to help you remember your password when you forget). Then click on Next

- Finally, click on Finish to complete the process

NOTE: You can also set a PIN lock on your Windows and to do this, follow the procedures above to creating a password.

Changing your Password

You may need to change your password for security purposes. To change your password

- From the start button, go to Settings
- Select Account and go to the Sign in options

- Go to password and click on Change

- In the next page that comes up, type your password and click on Next
- On the next page, type the new password and re-enter the new password. Then type in the password hint then click on Next

- On the final page, click on Finish

Creating a Picture Password

To create a picture password

- From the start button, go to Settings

- Select Account and go to the Sign in options
- Go to Picture password and click on Add
- Verify your identity by typing your password in the Create a picture password in the popup window

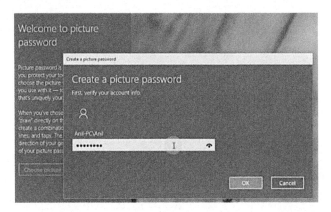

- Click on Choose picture in the Welcome to picture password dialogue box to select a picture

- In the Set up your gestures dialogue box, repeat the gestures you will like to use on the image and then click on Finish

Signing in with a Microsoft Account

The Microsoft account is one of the users' accounts in Windows. This gives access to taking advantage of the new features made available in Windows 10. To open a Microsoft account, you must have a valid e-mails account like Yahoo, Gmail Hotmail, etc. If you are using Windows 10 and you still don't have a Microsoft account, now let me teach you how to

create a Microsoft account by following the steps below:

To create or register a Microsoft account;

- From the start button, go to Settings
- Go to Accounts and Select Family & other people. Then click on Add someone else to this PC

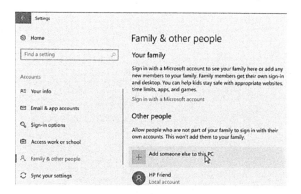

- Enter the e-mail address and click on Next. Since the e-mail address is not connected to Microsoft, select Sign in for a new one and click on Next

- Here on this page, fill in the required information and then click on Next.

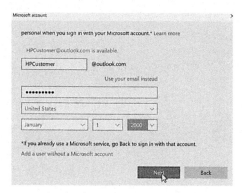

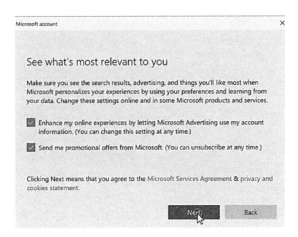

If you have followed the steps above accordingly, it means you now have a Microsoft account.

CHAPTER SIX

YOUR COMPUTER SECURITY IN WINDOWS 10

Computer security simply means the protection of your computer systems and information from harm, theft, and unauthorized use. Adequate security provisions have been made available with Windows 10. These securities functions include lock, sign out, sleep and shut down. These functions give you a personalized access to your computer systems. Below is a highlight of each of these security functions:

Locking the Computer

When you step away from your computer or you are leaving it for a while, it is important that you keep it secured by locking it.

The following steps describes how to lock your computer:

1. Using your keyboard shortcut key, press *Ctrl+Alt +Delete.*
2. Click Lock.
3. You can also lock your computer by clicking the start button and click the power option, then select lock.

Signing Out of the Computer

The following steps describes how to sign out of your computer:

1. Using your keyboard, press *Ctrl+Alt+Delete.*
2. Click Lock.
3. Click Sign Out. You will be automatically signed out of the computer.

Shutting Down the Computer

To shut down the computer, follow these steps:

1. Click the Start button on the Taskbar.
2. Click the Power icon.

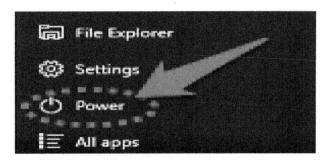

3. Click Shut down.

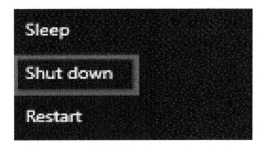

Activating Your Computer Sleep Mode

If you are going for a walk, you may place your computer to sleep instead of completely shutting it down. The following steps describes how to place your computer to sleep:

1. Click the Start button on the Taskbar.
2. Click the Power icon.
3. Click Sleep

CHAPTER SEVEN

SHORTCUT KEYS TO USING WINDOWS 10

In this chapter, I will be giving us some shortcut keys that will come in handy while working on your Windows 10. Don't forget time is life and I am sure you don't want to waste your time doing what you could have done for a short time at a longer period. For this reason, let's dive into the shortcuts for Windows 10

Classical Shortcuts

Shortcuts	Function
Windows button + L	To lock the screen
Alt + Tab	To move between open apps
Alt + F4	To close active apps
Ctrl + X	To cut selected item
Ctrl + C	To copy the selected item
Ctrl + V	To paste the selected item
Ctrl + A	To highlight all items

Ctrl + P	To print
Ctrl + Y	To redo an action
Ctrl + Z	To undo an action
Ctrl + Left arrow	To move the cursor to the beginning of the previous word
Ctrl + Right arrow	To move the cursor to the beginning of the next word
Ctrl + Up arrow	To move the cursor to the beginning of the previous paragraph
Ctrl + Alt+ Del	To show the Windows Security screen
Esc	To exit or close the current task

Accessibility Shortcuts

General

Shortcuts	Functions
Start button + U	To Start the Ease of Access Center
Left Alt + Left Shift + PrtSc	To switch High Contrast on or off
Left Alt + Left Shift + NumLock	To switch Mouse keys on or off
Hold Numlock for 5 seconds	To switch Toggle Keys on or off
Hold Right Shift for 8 seconds	To switch Filter keys on or off
Press Shift 5 times	To switch Sticky Keys on or off

Using the Magnifier

Shortcut	Functions
Windows key + Plus sign	To zoom in

Windows key + Minus sign	To zoom out
Ctrl + Alt + D	To switch to Docked mode
Ctrl + Alt + F	To switch to Full mode
Ctrl + Alt + I	For invert colors
Ctrl + Alt + L	To switch to Lens mode
Ctrl + Alt +R	To resize the lens
Ctrl + Alt +arrow keys	To move left, right, up and down
Windows key + Esc	To exit Magnifier

For using the Narrator

Shortcuts	Functions
Windows key + Enter	To start Narrator
Cap Lock + M	To start reading
Ctrl	To stop reading
Caps Lock + H	To read document

Caps Lock + W	To read window
Caps Lock + Page Up	To increase the volume of the Narrator's voice
Cap Lock + Page Down	To decrease the volume of the Narrator's voice
Cap Lock + Plus sign	To increase the speed of the Narrator's voice
Cap Lock + Minus sign	To decrease the speed of the Narrator's voice
Caps Lock + Esc	Exit Narrator

Communication shortcuts

Using the Calendar App

Shortcuts	Functions
Ctrl + N	To create a New event
Ctrl + S	To save or send an event
Ctrl + D	To delete an event

Using the Mail App

Shortcuts	Functions
Ctrl + M	To check for new mails
Ctrl + Q	To mark as read
Ctrl + U	To mark as Unread
Ctrl + N	To create a new message
Alt + I	To insert attachment
Alt + S	To send message

Desktop Shortcuts

Generals

Shortcuts	Functions
Windows key + A	To open the Action Center
Windows key + C	To launch Cortana
Windows key + D	To show Desktop
Windows key + H	To show Sharing options

Windows key + K	To connect wireless and audio devices
Windows key + S	To start a regular search
Windows key + the Comma sign	To peek at the Desktop
Windows key + PrtSc	To save a screenshot
Ctrl + Mouse scroll wheel	To resize the Desktop icons

For Task View and Taskbar

Shortcuts	Functions
Windows key + Tab	To launch the Task View
Windows key + Ctrl + D	To create a new Virtual Desktop
Windows key + Left or Right arrows	To switch in between Virtual Desktops
Windows key + Ctrl + F4	To close the current Virtual Desktop

Windows key + 1 to 9	To launch the app at the given position on the Taskbar

For Window display

Shortcuts	Functions
Windows key + Left arrow	To resize or snap the active window to the left part of the screen
Windows key + Right arrow	To resize or snap the active window to the right part of the screen
Windows key + Up arrow	To maximize the active window
Windows key + Shift + Up arrow	To stretch the window
Windows key + Down arrow	To minimize the active window
Windows key + M	To minimize all windows

| Windows key + Shift + M | To restore all windows |
| Windows key + Home | To minimize all windows except the active window |

File Explorer shortcuts

Shortcuts	Functions
Windows key + E	To launch the File Explorer
Alt	To use the Ribbon Key tips
Alt + D	To select the address bar
Alt + P	To display the previous pane
Alt + Enter	To show the properties of any selected file
Alt + Up arrow	To go one level in the directory structure

Alt + Left arrow	To show the previous folder
Alt + Right arrow	To show the next folder
Ctrl + Shift + N	To open a new window
Ctrl + N	To open a new window
Ctrl + E	To select the search box
Ctrl + W	To close the active window
Ctrl + Mouse scroll wheel	To resize the file and folder icon by using the view layout

The Microsoft Edge Shortcuts

For Navigation

Shortcuts	Functions
Alt + Home	To move to the Home page
Alt + Left arrow	To go back

Alt + Right arrow	To go forward
F5	To reload
Spacebar	To scroll down
Shift + Spacebar	To scroll up
Home	To move to the top of the page
End	To move to the bottom of the page
Ctrl + Plus sign	To zoom in
Ctrl + Minus sign	To zoom out
Ctrl + Zero	To reset the zoom level
Ctrl + N	To open a new browser window
Ctrl + P	To print the current webpage
Ctrl + Shift + P	To open a private browsing window

Ctrl + Shift + R	To activate the reading view
Ctrl + Shift + Del	To clear the browsing data
Shift + left click	To open a new window
Esc	To stop a page from loading

For Searching and Saving

Shortcuts	Functions
Ctrl + D	To save the current page to favorite
Ctrl + E	To search
Ctrl + F	To find a page
Ctrl + G	To open the Reading List
Ctrl + H	To open browsing history
Ctrl + I	To open your favorites

| Ctrl + J | To open downloads |
| Ctrl + L | To select the address bar |

For Tab Browsing

Shortcuts	Functions
Ctrl + 1 to 8	To move to a particular tab
Ctrl + 9	To move to the last tab
Ctrl + Tab	To move to the next tab
Ctrl + Shift + Tab	To move to the previous tab
Ctrl + K	To duplicate a tab
Ctrl + T	To open a new tab
Ctrl + W	To close a tab
Ctrl + Shift + T	To reopen the tab that was closed last

CHAPTER EIGHT

WINDOWS 10 TIPS AND TRICKS

Minimize all Windows Except the Active One

If your desktop screen has gotten too jam-packed with open windows, you can easily minimize them all except the one you are currently working in. Just click the title bar of the window you want to remain open to select it. After that, hold the mouse down and move the window back and forth quickly; shaking it, essentially. After a couple of quick shakes, all other open windows will be minimized, leaving only the one you have shaken open.

Open the Secret Start Menu

Basically, to get to the Start menu, you hit the Windows icon at the bottom left of the screen or on your keyboard. But more than this, 10 Windows includes a lesser-known second Start menu that makes gaining access to important features like the Control Panel, the Command Prompt, and the Task Manager much easier. You can access it two different ways, either by pressing the Windows key + X, or right click the Windows icon/Start button.

Create an event without opening the Calendar app

With the latest update of Windows 10, you can quickly add events to your Microsoft calendar directly from your Taskbar without actually having to open the calendar at all.

To get this done, follow these steps:

i.   On your Taskbar, click the box with the time and date at the bottom right corner.
ii. Click the date when you want to schedule an event.
iii. Enter the event name, time and location.
iv. Click save. The event should appear in your Calendar app Across Your Devices.

Figure Out How Much Space Apps are Taking Up

Computers start running slower as they grow short on space (memory). One quick way to speed them up may be to get rid of apps that take up more space than they should, especially if you do not frequently use them. To see how much space an app uses, navigate to Settings > System > Storage. Click on the drive you want to search (likely the local storage, "This PC"), and click Apps & games to see a list of apps installed on your computer and how much space they are taking up.

Get Rid of Ads in your Start Menu

When you run Windows 10 with default settings, you may sometimes see apps on the right side of your Start menu. Microsoft calls them *suggestions*, but they are actually ads for Windows Store apps you can buy.

To get rid of these, go to Settings > Personalization > Start. Toggle the setting called Show suggestions occasionally in Start to the off position.

Shut down background apps

Apps that run in the background can send notifications, receive

info, and stay updated, even when you are not using them. These apps usually suck your battery and your data, if you are connecting via a mobile hotspot.

To control which apps are running in the background and save some battery power and data, go to Settings > Privacy > Background apps. To stop all apps from running in the background, toggle *Let apps run in the background* to Off or, you can choose which apps to run in the background individually by going down the list on the same page.

Cut Down on Distractions with Focus Assist

It is always frustrating to try and get work done when

you keep getting interrupted with notifications. You can determine how many you get with Focus assist, a tool Windows 10 added in the

April 2018 update. You can set it up by going to *Settings > System > Focus assist.*

Choose from three options: *Off* (get all notifications from your apps and contacts), *Priority* (see only selected notifications from a priority list that you customize, and send the rest to your action center) and *Alarms only* (hide all notifications, except for alarms). You can also choose to automatically turn this feature on during certain hours, or when you are playing a game.

Malware Removal

Cyber security is always a great concern for Windows users. From this point of view, Microsoft keeps improving its own security tool to prevent your computer from being attacked. Windows Defender is such a tool which can be set up to block

malware attacks in real-time. Also, when there is a need, you can run it to perform an instant scan.

To turn Windows Defender on, type *Windows Defender* in Cortana search box and select Windows

Defender settings. Click Turn on Windows Defender Antivirus to make sure the real-time protection is on.

Sharing Files on Windows 10

Do you care to share files with your family and friends? I believe most users use USB devices to transfer, or send files by email. But Windows 10 offers you a more appropriate option to share files which is called *HomeGroup*.

Note: To create or join in a homegroup, your computer's network location must be set to Private.

Step 1.

Right-click Windows Start button and go to Settings. Next, go to Network & Internet > HomeGroup > Create a HomeGroup.

Step 2

Follow the wizard to choose what to share and set your own password.

Step 3

Click finish to complete and share password with your family for successful access.

Windows 10 Quick Tips

There are always Windows quick tips that can help you do anything a step ahead. Here are the most commonly used Windows 10 hidden features you should probably know.

1. Hold down the Shift key when dragging a file or folder to the Recycle Bin to delete it prematurely.
2. Hold down Alt and then double click on file or folder to open its Properties.
3. To open Command Prompt window, press Windows logo key + R at the same time and run CMD. Or you can type CMD in the address bar of File Explorer and press Enter.
4. To quickly create a shortcut, hold down Ctrl + Shift and then drag and drop the file or folder icon in the desired destination folder.
5. Press Ctrl + Shift and then right-click on the Taskbar. You will then see the option to Exit Explorer in the last row.

CONCLUSION

With the rate at which the world is changing with respect to technology, it is expedient as an individual to get yourself acquainted with Windows 10 on your desktop. Laptops and tablet devices. There are a lot of features embedded in the Windows 10 and I am sure by now you have truly gone through this user guide; you must have discovered these wonderful features Windows 10 and how they can be used in your day to day activities that involve the use of a computer.

If you truly desire to make the best use of your computers, Windows 10 is specifically made for you.

I wish you all the best of luck as you begin to explore the world of Windows 10

Printed in Great Britain
by Amazon